Mark Palmer

HOPE REALISTIC

Aspirations for Survivors of Traumatic Brain Injury

ISBN: 1-4392-4451-0
ISBN-13: 9781439244517

Visit www.booksurge.com to order additional copies.

Acknowledgements

This booklet has been written with passion to help those with TBI—and others—find the courage and support to live their lives to the fullest by accepting their "new normal." From this beginning, I hope they will strive to be a little better every day, while appreciating every step of the journey.

I want to say a special thanks to my wife, for without her encouragement, love and support, I would not have made or continued to make the decision to be the best that I can be. It is a decision that I still must make every day. Thank-you also to our sons for never questioning the disruptions to their lives that resulted from my injury. I am truly blessed with a supportive family—a family whose suffering was increased as a result of my drive to return to my pre-injury "normal."

Thank you also to Frank Lagatutta, M.D., who, 31 years after the injury, led me to the discovery of my new normal. As a result of his leadership, my hopes and dreams became realistic. I have been able to improve the quality of life for my wife, our kids, and myself. I will be better able to enjoy our grandkids.

This book would not exist without the encouragement of Kristi Cooper White, Jane Szczepaniak, Sara Soltau, Karen Brownlee, and Eric Schmitz. Thank you.

Table of Contents

Author's Perspective

I have developed this work as the result of experiencing traumatic injury from five different perspectives:

As the injured who suffered a TBI after a broadside collision with a Detroit city bus. I went into a coma, survived 15 surgeries, a dozen or so grand mal seizures, scores of shoulder dislocations, and, most recently, 14 years of self-referred physical rehabilitation to reach my highest level of physical functioning.

As a family member offering support to a son and daughter-in-law managing the care of their son with Aplastic anemia—a journey that took them through prognosis, treatment, a long wait, recovery and an evolving "new normal." I am proud to say that this family has successfully created a new life for themselves by accepting and building upon their "new normal."

As the family member in charge of managing care for a brother who suffered a crippling decline in health, a mistaken diagnosis, disagreement among caregivers, and a dysfunctional support group until arriving at the correct diagnosis, proper care, and a long recovery from Guillain-Barré Syndrome. My brother lost almost all muscle function and had to spend 42 days in ICU on a ventilator. He is now building his life from his new normal.

As a family member offering support to others going through open-heart surgery, depression, and other major life challenges.

As a coach to survivors and their families through each step of the journey of recovery from traumatic illness or injury. As coach, my goal is to encourage the building of realistic hopes from "the new normal," helping everyone involved to recognize and appreciate each achievement, no matter how small.

As a result of these experiences I have learned that, while there is no such thing as a "return to normal" following a traumatic injury, it is certainly possible to live a great life and to pursue realistic dreams based on being the best you can be. The process begins with accepting where and who and how you are right now.

Hard Realities about TBI

This booklet focuses on Traumatic Brain Injury, or TBI, although there are many types of traumatic injuries that this information also applies to.

The National Center for Injury Prevention and Control estimates that 1.1 million people in the United States sustain a traumatic brain injury (TBI) every year. Of this number, 50,000 die. Another 235,000 are hospitalized, and the rest are treated in an emergency room and released. But discharge from the hospital is not an indication that all is well with TBI victims. Population-based studies have found that people with TBI have an increased risk of death by suicide 3-4 times greater than the general population—a fact that reflects the many ongoing challenges TBI survivors face.

Compounding these sobering statistics, thousands of dedicated young men and women will return from Iraq and Afghanistan suffering from traumatic brain injury—as many as 300,000, or 19%, according to a 2008 report by the Institute of Medicine. Like their civilian peers, they will be met by doctors, family and friends tragically unprepared to provide support—or even to realize that support is needed. Instead, TBI victims and their families will hope and pray for a "return to normal"—a return to yesterday—unaware that this hope is unrealistic, if not impossible. Worse, the discrepancy between what is hoped for and what is possible will create frustration, disappointment, bitterness, and despair.

But it doesn't have to be this way. TBI survivors and their families—and all those who have suffered a life-threatening illness or injury—can look forward to a bright future, so long as they are prepared to build that future on who and what they are today—not who they might have been before the injury or illness.

Anatomy of a Traumatic Injury

A traumatic brain injury or other life-threatening illness affects a lot of people. At the same time, a lot of different players affect the outcome for the person who has been injured.

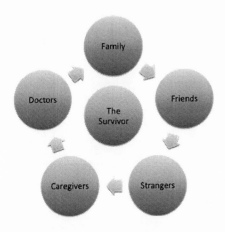

On the following page is a matrix that identifies many of these participants and summarizes the journey and interactions that each of them is likely to take from the moment of the injury to the day a survivor returns home.

The matrix is intended as a tool to facilitate discussions among the participants on a survivor's support team. From these discussions, I hope that all who are affected by a traumatic injury will find a common set of realistic dreams and a shared understanding of the process taking place as they work to support their loved one's recovery.

Anatomy of a Traumatic Injury

Timeline ───

PARTY	INJURY	SURGERY/COMA	HOSPITAL
PATIENT	Probably unaware or unable to participate	Probably unaware or unable to participate	Confused, as if in a dream. Embarrassed; no privacy. Afraid, powerless, vulnerable. humiliated, angry.
FAMILY	Fearful, sympathetic, concerned, angry.	Fearful, overwhelmed. Physically/emotionally drained. What will happen next? In limbo. Shifts in familial roles. Angry.	Relief: "out of the woods." Exhausted, dealing with insurance;, financial strain. Intense emotions. Monitoring doctors to ensure quality care. Juggling responsibilities. Angry.
FRIENDS	Fearful, nervous, sympathetic, concerned.	Sympathetic, fearful, concerned. .	Relief: "out of the woods." Supportive, bringing gifts and food.
STRANGERS	*Strangers at Hospital in Like Circumstances* Sympathetic, scared, nervous.	*Strangers at Hospital in Like Circumstances* Sympathetic, scared, nervous.	*Strangers at Hospital in Like Circumstances* Sympathetic, scared, nervous.
CAREGIVERS	*Nurses - Technicians - Aids* Care.	*Nurses - Technicians - Aides* Care.	*Nurses - Technicians - Aides* Care.
DOCTORS	*Triage* Care	*Specialist* Care	*Attending* Focused on success, doing all they can do.

©Focus, LLC, Mark Palmer

REHAB	HOME	LIFE EVER AFTER: A CHOICE
Hopeful, validated. Somebody is worse. Learning more each day. Feelings of "why me?" Angry.	Disengaged. Estranged from self. Socially isolated. A burden to self and others. Susceptible to negative comments. Worried. Can't fulfill obligations. Purposeless. Angry.	ACCEPT: Adapt, learn to live with your new self, become self-sufficient, be the BEST you can be.
		EXIST: Wishing for the past
		NOT ACCEPT: Give up. Isolated, angry, depressed, suicidal, dependent, suicidal.
Empathetic. Keeping track of progress. Making critical decisions. Facing financial strain. Working double-duty to fulfill family obligations. Angry.	Disappointed. Want things the way they were. Overly controlling and protective. Still facing financial strain. Angry.	ACCEPT: Move forward. Continue to be supportive.
		EXIST: Wishing for the past
		NOT ACCEPT: Anger. Disassociation. Divorce.
Check in occasionally. Moving on with their lives.	Visits dwindle. Feel uncomfortable, guilty.	ACCEPT: Move forward. Continue to be supportive.
		EXIST: Wishing for the past
		NOT ACCEPT Most move on and disappear.
Strangers at Rehab in Like Circumstances	**General Public in Unlike circumstances**	**General Public in Unlike circumstances**
Sympathetic, scared, nervous.	Misunderstand, stare, judge, feel superior. Sometimes offended by what is perceived as inappropriate behavior. Not available to form new friendships.	Misunderstand, stare, judge, feel superior. Sometimes offended by what is perceived as inappropriate behavior. Not available to form new friendships.
Therapist - Aides	**Home Care**	**Family - Friends**
Care. Bond in the image of a new caring "relationship"	Supportive, yet highlight patient's lack of independence	Reactive
Rehab	**All**	**All**
Reactive	Reactive	Reactive

Realistic Hope

Realistic dreams—dreams that are achievable—provide wonderful incentive for living. They make life an adventure. They offer a reason to start each day as if it were the beginning of the rest of your life. They infect dreamers with the passion to live for the enjoyment of today, and give them a never-ending supply of options for starting over again tomorrow.

Unrealistic dreams—dreams that are never achievable— are exactly the opposite. They make life a series of disappoint- ments ending in failure. They rob dreamers of energy and pride in their incremental progress. They infect dreamers with a sense of futility that makes each day just another one to get through, hoping for a miracle, wishing for what can never be—or, as is often the case, for what was.

Realistic dreams give people a sense of purpose and a way to measure progress. Unrealistic dreams give people a sense of hopelessness and the feeling that, no matter how hard they try, they will never succeed.

But how does one know the difference? And what about the countless people who have achieved the unthinkable, who have done what even the experts said could "never" be done? Where would they be if they'd listened to people who told them to "be realistic"?

I suggest that when we look at those who have accom- plished "the impossible," we are seeing the cumulative result of the achievement of many smaller dreams, rather than the grandiose accomplishment of a single super-sized dream. Just as America succeeded in putting a man on the moon by first putting a spaceship in orbit, then a chimp in orbit, then a man in orbit, and so on, success builds upon success. Failures give an opportunity for pause and re-evaluation. By making steady, incremental progress, major milestones are achieved.

Coming Home

On a crisp January day in 1965 when I was 15 years old, I was released from Bon Secours Hospital in Grosse Pointe, Michigan. My parents and I were celebrating—my father and I in the front seat, my mother leaning forward from the back seat to wrap her arms protectively around me every time we crossed an intersection. I had survived a car accident, a depressed skull fracture, and a coma. I had not been expected to live. If I'd lived, I had not been expected to regain consciousness. If I regained consciousness, I had not been expected to function. I had invalidated all the prognostications. It seemed that everything was OK. My parents clearly believed that if they could just get through the nerve-wracking drive home, the nightmare would be over.

Little did we understand that, really, only the hospital stay was behind us. Looking back 45 years, 15 surgeries, and endless rounds of physical therapy, pain therapy, and various other therapies later, I now realize that coming home was only the beginning of a much longer ordeal—a lifelong ordeal that continues to this day. I have learned that this is likely to be true for most TBI survivors, as well.

Yet I have also realized that the gap between what I and my caregivers hoped for me and what we should have been hoping for instead—ironically—made my journey more difficult. Unrealistic hopes of what I could achieve resulted in additional layers of trauma and even physical pain and disability as we denied reality in order to pursue "being normal."

The truth is that, like me, every TBI survivor has been granted a second chance at life. A blessing has been bestowed upon us. It is my hope that the information you are about to read here will help every survivor—and every caregiver—to grab a hold of this second chance with all the passion, gratitude, and enthusiasm that life deserves.

The journey most often begins with a shock...

THE JOURNEY

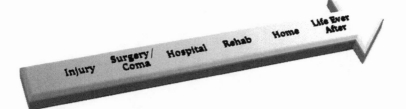

Injury — Surgery/Coma — Hospital — Rehab — Home — Life Ever After

Injury - Your Loved One is Injured

You receive a call and learn that a loved one has been injured, had a stroke, or has a grave illness, and you are the logical one to make the tough decisions with regard to medical care. Perhaps you are the parent, the spouse, a sibling, or dear friend, now in charge of a situation for which you most likely have never had any training.

A flood of questions runs through your mind: will the injured live, what will the treatment be, how long will it take, and when will your loved one be able to come home and return to normal? You change your schedule, transfer responsibilities, and head off to the hospital.

On the way you call friends and family members to inform them of the situation: the triage doctors are attempting to stabilize your loved one while making decisions about the best specialists to involve as soon as he or she is stabilized. You walk into the emergency room, shocked to see the physical state of the one you love.

The triage team informs you of the conditions and what specialists will be involved. The specialists, in turn, inform you about the treatment options. You do not get answers to the questions you have; in fact, in many situations the answers do not exist. The medical team has helped to focus your concern on saving your loved one's life.

Friends and other family members begin to arrive at the hospital. They want to know what's happening. They want to know what you're going to do. This is an excruciating time: the life of a loved one is at-risk; decisions are forced upon you that you feel unqualified to make; people ask questions you cannot answer—even the doctors cannot answer. Nevertheless, you decide on a course of treatment and the patient is rushed off to receive the chosen medical care.

Injury - My story

My family was getting ready for dinner when my parents received a phone call informing them that I—their 15-year-old son—had been in a car accident 60 miles from home. I had been taken to the nearest Detroit hospital; initial review indicated a broken right arm. My parents were told that the arm should be set; that they could complete the paperwork upon arrival and take me home.

My parents thought I had gone skiing, not to Detroit. They would never have given me permission to go to downtown Detroit with a newly licensed driver on a day where snow had turned to freezing rain. They were upset. I was fortunate to have only a broken arm. I should have known better. I would be punished!

Upon their arrival at the hospital, they were informed of the possibility that I might have a head injury. The doctors had decided to keep me in the hospital. My parents found themselves 60 miles from home with no change of clothes, and their son with a possible head injury. I spoke to them, but made no sense. They were ready to panic.

Despite a packed, inner-city emergency room and the competing claims on their attention made by incoming gunshot victims, handcuffed prisoners, and others in need of medical care, the doctors were awesome—able to diagnose a severely depressed skull fracture, with blood clots on the brain creating an urgent need for surgery. My parents were soon informed that arrangements had been made for surgery at a hospital better equipped for the procedure. Time was of the essence; an ambulance was on its way.

By the time I arrived at the next hospital I was in a coma. Medical support staff greeted us prepared to execute a single set of orders: prep me for surgery, quickly, as a distinguished neurosurgeon was waiting in the operating room.

My parents were ill-equipped to hear that I was likely to die on the operating table. If I survived the surgery they could expect me to be severely handicapped.

In a medical emergency, the victim's needs are well-attended to. It is the family's needs that are neglected. The following suggestions are meant to help families and friends get through the crisis immediately following the accident, injury, or diagnosis of illness:

Help those closest to the injured:

Establish someone to be in charge. Sometimes this choice is obvious: the parent of a minor, the spouse of an adult. This individual should pick one or two others to help him or her make decisions based on the best information available. This is not a time for consensus decision-making. Unfortunately, whatever decisions you make are likely to spark disagreement. You simply won't be able to please everybody.

As the one in charge, have the **courage** to tell those who second-guess you, "Thank you for your input." If you are one of the other friends or family members, please respect the decisions of the lead family member. Offer to help in any way you can. Provide input if asked, but please do not criticize the decisions made.

Inform the medical staff of the family member in charge. Let them know that this is the person through whom information should flow. Hold the doctors and medical staff accountable for providing honest answers to your questions to the extent that answers exist. Don't be afraid to get disagreeing members of the medical team to explain their differences, because it will be up to you to decide the course of treatment.

The early stages of the journey are almost certain to be a struggle: the doctors speak about saving or stabilizing a life, and you want answers about returning to normal. You want answers that do not exist; they need decisions on the treatment options presented. Frustrating as it is, family members and friends have to accept that, for now, there are no answers to some of their most burning questions.

Injury - Support

Establish a communication plan to manage inquiries from friends and family who will reach out to help. Otherwise, the sheer volume of calls can become overwhelming for the lead family member. I suggest you name a person to be in charge of communication, so that the lead family member only has to communicate with him or her. This communications coordinator can then see that a website is established, emails go out, or daily calls are returned to keep **concerned friends and family members informed.**

Give well-wishers a job. They want to help. The medical community is taking care of the injured; it's the family members spending days and nights at the hospital who need help. Name a third person to organize well-wishers and give his or her contact information to the communications coordinator so that those who want to help can be given a job. Let well-wishers walk the dogs, feed the cats, collect the mail, pay the bills, clean the house, prepare the meals, return phone calls, build a website, organize a fundraiser, etc.

Medical bills will soon begin arriving in volume, and many will sound urgent—adding unnecessary stress at a time when stress is already running high. Ask someone to organize and consolidate the bills and identify the ones that may actually need prompt attention.

To family and friends, make sure that your presence adds value, rather than merely generates additional questions. Offer to help organize or execute any of the above.

Although this list of "help" items is not intended to be inclusive, knowing who is in charge of decision-making, who is in charge of communications, and who is organizing the help, will make this difficult journey a bit easier.

Surgery or Coma - The Wait

While waiting to see if your loved one will live, you find yourself sitting with strangers who are in similar situations. You reach out to each other offering welcome, nonjudgmental support.

Everyone—family, friends, strangers, caregivers and doctors—is focused on saving the injured one's life. Prayers, hope, and dreams, too, are focused on survival as you wait for news.

While you are waiting, you—the close family members—have a few minutes to think about yourselves—then are likely to feel guilty for doing so. Yet the truth is that your lives probably have been changed by the accident as dramatically as the patient's life has changed. It is natural to spend some time considering this.

Assume that the unconscious victim can hear and feel—so talk, touch, and express your love. (For the same reasons, take conflict or negative conversations out of the patient's hearing!) Still, your demonstrations of caring don't have to be ceaseless. It's OK to take time to handle your own life. Let the injured know how many and how much people care and, at the same time, discourage a constant stream of visitors.

Finally you get the wonderful news that your loved one has survived surgery, or come out of a coma. The initial treatment plans were a success. You breathe relief.

Friends and family members can't wait to surround the survivor and see with their own eyes how he or she is. Well-wishers ask, "Is he going to be all right?" Doctors answer "Yes, he will live." Well-wishers hear, "He will be 'his old self' again."

The reality is that the injured will never "be his old self again." This is the time to begin building realistic dreams based on a "new normal" that has not yet been defined.

Surgery or Coma - My Family's Story

It was midnight. They had been told that their son would probably not be alive in a few hours. Other family members were 60 miles away. Filling that vacuum, strangers and hospital caregivers reached out to give my parents whatever support they could.

The doctors exceeded expectations: many hours and five pints of blood later, my parents were informed that I had survived. I was stable, although I remained in a coma. The doctor recommended round-the-clock nursing care. A very cautious "wait-and-see" was the only answer he could give my parents who were desperate to know my prognosis. He was prepared to go back to surgery on a moment's notice, if necessary. He had given the nurses my care instructions.

Relieved that I had survived, my parents' concern shifted to wondering "how handicapped?" Distant relatives living near the hospital offered a place to stay. Relatives from 60 miles away started taking turns to visit, while I lay in a coma with 24-hour nursing care. Hospital roommates would recover and be discharged, new ones would come. Each departing patient left a phone number my parents could call for support. Strangers reached out to comfort my parents.

Seventeen days later, I awoke from the coma with far less handicap than had been expected. I was paralyzed on my left side, my right arm in a cast. My ability to speak was poor, but improving rapidly. My parents were so relieved that they pushed hard for the going home criteria from the doctor. The answer was straightforward: I must be able to eat, void, and walk on my own. The family's mission was clear...

Surgery or Coma - My Story

As a loved one or caregiver, a nurse or physician, your support makes a huge difference to the quality of life of a survivor.

I owe my own survival from TBI to the care and support I received from a wide network of individuals—some of whom I didn't even know. Distant relatives we had never met opened their home to my parents, providing a place for them to stay while I was in a hospital far from home. Virtual strangers, they helped my parents survive a crisis better than known family members could have and, as a result, became a cherished part of our lives for 40 years.

I also had exceptional round-the-clock private nursing care—nurses who read aloud to me every get-well card I received. They made me believe that my survival was important—even while I remained comatose. One hundred and eighteen of my 122 paper route customers sent me at least one card—all of which were read to me, although I was in a coma. In fact, this is one of the few things I still remember from the coma.

Even from the depths of my unconsciousness, I perceived that I was surrounded by family, friends, doctors, nurses, paper route customers, and untold strangers who were focused on a single unconditional purpose: that I might live. Their unified support gave me the strength to come out of the coma. Although I have no logical way of explaining how this information was presented to me, I know I faced two options: stay in this safe comatose place, a place without challenges, or make the decision to return to consciousness and fight to be the best I could be.

It was clear even at the time that the decision to fight was the harder choice; yet the support I felt from everyone who was anxiously waiting for me to live—just live—let me know that my decision mattered; that I was wanted among the living, unconditionally.

This work is a plea for all of us to give the thing we already know how to give to our loved ones who have been injured, who are ready to move on with the rest of their lives. They are asking for our unconditional love and acceptance for who they are now.

The Hospital Stay - Recovery Begins

The immediate crisis is over: your loved one will live. The first feelings are joy, elation, relief, and gratitude.

The doctors celebrate success. Their treatments saved a life. They will now move on to the next critical patient. It is time for the survivor, his family, and friends to move on to their next job, as well.

When a survivor returns to consciousness, he inevitably has questions: What just happened to me? Will I be the same as I used to be? If not, what will my life be like now? When can I go home? Why me?

It is at this crucial point that survivors can take their first steps toward either acceptance or denial of their new reality. They face the challenge of accepting their "new normal" in every relationship, role and responsibility. It is likely that all have been changed.

The entire support team's assistance may be necessary to help the injured arrive at the answer: "No, you will not be the same as you used to be; the same as yesterday. Even if you regain 100 percent of your previous functioning, you have had a life-altering experience. You, and we, have been changed. You will never be the same again because, at the very least, you will have learned something. You are a wonderful individual moving forward into the future. Who knows what experiences await you? You can progress from here only by starting with who you are now."

Realistic hope can begin now—working to recover enough to be discharged from the hospital and admitted to rehabilitation. From rehabilitation your goal will be to become self-sufficient enough to go home.

Hospital Stay - My Story

As my awareness increased I listened to the stories of what had happened to me and began to assemble what memories I could from the coma.

Although I was paralyzed on my left side and my right arm was in a cast, the fact that I was conscious meant to me that I was heading back to "normal." Although I couldn't speak clearly, I wasn't troubled by it. My mind knew what it wanted to say; the fact that others couldn't understand me wasn't my problem! I wanted my glasses so I could see.

Now that I had emerged from my coma, my family's focus was on getting me home. It is only now, in retrospect, that I can see that their urgency was unrealistic. They hung on to the doctor's criteria: eat, void, and walk on my own. Their mission was clear, but it ignored medical reality and my own state of denial.

In the meantime, I was also experiencing tremendous guilt. I'd gotten in an accident being somewhere I wasn't supposed to be. I'd betrayed my parents' trust, caused them anguish and financial hardship, and though no one ever spoke about it, I now see that guilt was among the factors driving me to minimize my injuries and "get well" as soon as possible.

Days later, I was discharged with instructions to find a neurosurgeon close to home. After all, I did have a 4-inch hole in my skull that needed a metal plate. I was to "take it easy" until we found the next doctor. So...

The Hospital Stay - Providing Support

As part of the survivor's support team, your challenge is to provide realistic encouragement, not denial or false encouragement. False encouragement disqualifies you as a credible supporter. Forty-five years later, I can still recall a well-intended but very hurtful experience:

I'd been told by a doctor that one requirement to discharge was the demonstrated ability to feed myself. Although I was paralyzed on the left side and my right arm was in a cast, my family was gung-ho on getting me to demonstrate this skill. Several of them stood around my bed as breakfast oatmeal was placed in front of me. My first attempt at getting the food in my mouth landed the oatmeal on my stomach. My family shouted, "That was good!" My second attempt hit my shoulder, and my family shouted, "That was better!" My third attempt hit my cheek; they shouted, "That was your best one yet!"

I felt like a monkey in a cage, surrounded by non-credible coaches. Although the objective was to eat, they were praising me for failure. It was an unrealistic hope that on that day I would be able to feed myself. What if the hope had only been to hold a spoon in my hand?

A small difference, yet the difference between failure and success.

It is very hard not to give your loved ones undeserved praise. Yet that only distances you from their reality. I plead with you to give support for the frustration they are experiencing, along with the encouragement to try again.

On To Rehab...and Then

When a survivor moves to rehabilitation, he or she may feel hopeful about their prospects for recovery and grateful that their condition is not as bad as others they see around them. They may feel empowered with the new skills and abilities they acquire each day. On the other hand, they may feel angry and frustrated that they have to relearn skills that once were automatic, or that their progress is not as rapid or as steady as they expect. Occasionally they may be overwhelmed by feelings of injustice ("Why me?"), hopelessness, and despair.

Family members are affected by the survivor's emotional state—whether positive or negative—and also bring their own fears and expectations to bear on the survivor. In addition, family members are dealing with insurance paperwork, facing financial strain, struggling to return to work or to balance the needs of other family members for time and attention, etc. Family members can feel stretched to the breaking point, and may feel anger and resentment as a result.

At long last, the survivor is discharged from rehab and comes home. Today is a day of celebration. Everyone believes that the ordeal is almost over. Now life can return to normal.

For survivors, the initial sense of elation is often followed by estrangement—from yourself, your former life, your family and friends. Socially isolated, you may begin to feel like a burden to yourself and others. You may be angry. In fact, you may rage at your lot in life; yet the only people you can express your anger to are the very ones you depend on for support. You may be sensitive to negative comments—or even looks—from family, friends, and strangers. You worry what will become of you. What will your life be like, what will your future hold, what will your purpose be? How will you continue to "earn" your caregivers' love? How will you "pay your own way," "carry your own weight"?

Family members, too, frequently experience disappointment after the initial relief of the homecoming. They are frustrated that a return to "pre-event normal" is not forthcoming. They may have unrealistic expectations that the survivor "isn't trying," or is "giving in to depression" when in fact the survivor is simply struggling to accept her current reality. In addition, family members are struggling with finances, household management, and all their "pre-event" responsibilities, along with caring for the survivor. They too may feel anger and resentment.

Now that their loved one has been released from medical care, many friends will feel the need to move on with their own lives. Friends who are distressed by the survivor's new "normal" are likely to feel guilty in his presence and stop visiting. Only those who can accept the survivor as he is are able to continue the friendship.

At this point, strangers are no longer likely to be a source of support. Instead, they are those members of the general public who stare, pass judgment, perhaps feel superior, or perhaps are offended at behavior they deem inappropriate. Their comments and stares can be hurtful to survivors and family members.

Home...a New Beginning

Whether you are a TBI survivor, a veteran from Iraq, a paraplegic from a car accident, or the survivor of a life-threatening illness, you have traveled a long journey to return home with high expectations. Your friends and family have endured many anxious moments awaiting your arrival.

Yet you are about to discover that the arrival home is the beginning of an even longer ordeal, not the sought-after ending. This is true for your family members, as well. They have weathered the acute crisis; now the chronic one begins. They know how much they feared losing you; but they, like you, don't necessarily know how to move forward. So you need each other. You have the chance to build a new life together—from a new starting point. It can be an amazing, miraculous road you travel together, but it will take a lot of understanding and patience from all.

I was meeting with a depressed TBI survivor, who told me that the most significant challenge he was facing was that "My daughter lost her Dad," implying that he was not the same person after his injury. I asked him, "Have you given her a chance to fall in love with her new Dad?"

When I ran into him a couple of weeks later, he was confident and happy. I inquired, "So...?" He answered, "I did, and she did."

The path we have to travel can be so rewarding if we give it a chance.

...Home - My Story

The first day home I was in a fog. I look back on how I felt that day and cannot believe how out of touch I was with reality. Yet I was convinced that I did have a clear grasp of my situation. Although I could not feed or dress myself, speech was difficult, and no one could understand me—nor I them—I nevertheless believed that I was just a few days away from my pre-accident normal. I had been lucky. I was fine. After all, there were others a lot worse off than myself.

The reality was that I had been discharged with my entire head in a bandage that covered a four-inch hole in my skull covered only by skin. Any puncture would go directly into my recently repaired brain.

My sister was moved to my second-floor bedroom, so that I could be stationed right next to my parents' room. I was not allowed to use the bathroom without supervision. My right arm was in a cast, my left side weak from having been paralyzed.

That first day home, friends and family members stopped by, were allowed to take a look and chat for a few minutes, and then were directed elsewhere. Each and every one congratulated me on my arrival home and my return to life as usual.

As the day ended, I really had no idea of what I had been through—or what lay before me. My accident, recovery, rehab, and homecoming seemed to have happened in the background; the events were real but I could not touch them. All of the celebration around me said that now everything must be good. The ordeal was over, I was OK, and things would soon be as they were before the accident.

Now I know that homecoming is one of the most difficult times for the family.

My message to everyone involved in this journey—survivors, families, friends, caregivers, doctors and the general public—is that we must recognize that our job is not over when our loved one returns home. Though we all may want to breathe a collective sigh of relief and turn our attention to other matters, the fact is that our family and friends still need our help, love and support. My advice is as follows:

- Maintain the communication plan created at the time of injury. The family does not need the burden of 30 phone calls a day.
- Establish someone to be in charge of scheduling - the caregivers, friends, and family who all want to visit; the appointments with doctors, therapists, etc.
- Call before you visit - arrange your visit with the person in charge of scheduling.
- Making a meal is not necessarily a good thing. Seeing that meals are covered through the one in charge of arranging meals is a wonderful thing. A kitchen full of meals that are not on the current diet is a liability.
- Gifts are not necessarily a good thing. The best gift is time spent with the survivor and caregivers once they have had a chance to establish their routine.

- The true gift is friendship and interest over time. It is way too easy to get on with our lives absent the injured. A 15-minute visit every quarter has far more value than an hour visit the week they come home from the hospital.

- Establish a relationship with an internist, family practitioner, or other primary care physician, who will be in charge of the survivor's care and act as a "gatekeeper," to oversee care from many different specialists.

Life Ever After

You, the survivor, are isolated—stuck at home, surrounded by your limitations, which may seem overwhelming. Never having traveled this road before, you may lack the faith and confidence that seem necessary for you to build a new "life ever after." Your family may feel the same way. "Will this work? Can I do this?" You may all be asking yourselves similar questions.

I invite you all to try the same answer:

Have the courage to dream small. Begin again to build realistic dreams. You don't get there by flipping a switch. You get there by nurturing a passion for life that encourages you to strive to be a little better, in some way, every day.

From my perspective, the accomplishment of major milestones—what some might even call "the unachievable"—is the result of:

- A succession of little dreams, the achievement of which gradually accumulates into a much bigger accomplishment
- A realistic view of today's challenges, which becomes a baseline for measuring subsequent accomplishments
- A passion to live for today, fulfilling small dreams to provide energy for the next day's challenges
- The confidence to live life according to one's own dreams, not the dreams of others—in other words, the confidence to be oneself

- A small group of supportive family and friends who are willing to accept survivors as they are, limitations and all

No matter what our injury or trauma, we all are entitled to realistic dreams. We are not and cannot be the same as yesterday. Although we do not know the limits of our eventual accomplishments, we do know that we can be a little better tomorrow than we are today. And the pursuit of that dream is the reason for living.

Here we were, believing I'd been "cured," as if I'd just recovered from the flu. We began to build our lives around the unrealistic expectation that everything was just like before. I accepted the mission to prove to the world that I was "normal." None of us had been trained—or even briefed—to work through the issues we would face. All the members of our household faced a terrible mismatch in expectations.

The overriding desire was to be like yesterday. But that cannot happen. In the meantime, mismatched expectations wore us out. "Why me?" was asked by every member of the household. "Why is the injured feeling bad? Don't they appreciate how much I've done for them?" "Why are my caregivers feeling bad? They're not the ones who are injured; I am! No, wait, I am okay."

Teachers felt sorry for me, so they passed me with As and Bs so that I could graduate from high school. My senior English classmates would take bets on my score on the weekly spelling tests. Would it be 5 out of 30, or 8 out of 30?

Hearing these stories, one might think it must have been obvious that I was not the same as before my accident. Yet it wasn't obvious to me. I was busy living up to the promise that everything was fine. Only over time did I discover how impaired I was.

I was 100% focused on making the injury positive. I was in denial, masquerading as acceptance. Seizures, surgeries, pain, and physical limitations all were just normal, I told myself. I had not accepted my brain injury; I had made the decision to prove to the world that I was not impaired in anyway. I was trying to achieve an unrealistic dream.

I could have avoided most, if not all, of these complications had I paid proper respect to my new normal.

My family's desire for me to be my old self was a double-edged sword. To meet their expectations, I did not ever use my injury as an excuse not to accomplish a given task. Yet, I learned to accept unnecessary pain and disruption as part of my norm, while foolishly kidding myself that I was the only one in pain.

Choices To Be Made

There are three options that confront each person with a brain injury and each of his friends and family members:

Giving up (easy): After all, you will never return to pre-injury normal

Existing, or refusing to choose (hard): Wishing for a pre-accident normal that will never be

Acceptance (hardest): Striving to be the best you can be, beginning with where you are now.

Choosing among these options is a task that must be made every day—and sometimes many times a day. Acceptance is a complex issue, involving three main areas of life in which we must learn its value: self, situation, and society.

Self. Learning to accept ourselves is one of the most difficult tasks we will ever accomplish. We must learn to gratefully accept our own unique personality, strengths, skills, and limitations.

Situation. We also must gratefully accept our current lot in life, especially the consequences of our decisions. In my own case, I was so busy "making the best" of my situation that I didn't realize how completely in denial I was of my physical limitations. I have since learned that my physical limitations weren't fixed, or permanent; but, ironically, I couldn't change them until I first acknowledged them. In my own case, it was my pride that got in the way, compounding my difficulties and delaying my eventual progress.

Society. We must not only accept ourselves and our situations, we must also learn to accept society—by which I mean the wide variety of "others" we encounter, including strangers that stare or pass judgment, without even considering that possibility of trauma or other impairments. Whether you are the survivor of a traumatic injury, or the friend or family member of a survivor, your relationship will present personal growth challenges for you. But we will never know the full possibilities of our relationships with others unless we commit to accepting them as they are.

ACCEPTANCE

Acceptance - It Is Important

Acceptance, like forgiveness, is easier to talk about than to achieve. I've learned that even though we may think we have accepted our "new normal," or our present reality, life has a way of showing us where this is simply not the case...where we have more "acceptance" work to do.

True acceptance is not approval but it is the only starting point for real transformation. Just as an alcoholic can only begin to recover by accepting that he is indeed an alcoholic, so too our recovery from traumatic injury begins with accepting the reality of our current condition. Unwelcome or hateful as it may be, it is the starting place for our "new normal."

A couple of experiences close together allowed me to begin to understand the impact my denial had on my family:

- I came home one day to find the lawn mowed. My wife informed me that she had hired a landscaper, as she could not stand to watch or listen to me experience and complain about the pain associated with mowing the lawn.

- One day she asked me a simple question, "If you are in this much pain at 47, what will you be like at 57?"

For the first time, I realized the pain that my wife was experiencing watching me pretend to be normal.

With her encouragement, I set out in search of help. As a result, I have come to realize that my wife and family have experienced as much, if not more, trauma than I myself: Witnessing seizures is far more traumatic than having them. Pulling shoulders back into place is far more traumatic than dislocating them. Sitting in the surgical waiting room is much more uncomfortable than being on the table.

Acceptance - The Beginning of Recovery

Fourteen years ago—31 years after the accident—my doctor made an offhand comment that changed my life. He said, "With personal commitment to being a little better every day, you should be able to compensate for most of your brain damage."

My mind reeled. "Brain damage? What brain damage? I'm normal, aren't I?"

After I recovered from the shock, I realized I had never accepted the truth about my situation. From that day forward I did. I began to build my life based on my "new normal," which included brain damage. I now see that it was this acceptance that gave me a realistic dream of reducing pain and improving my lifestyle.

From that moment I began spending my energies trying to be a little better every day. I am proud to say today that my quality of life is much better than it was 14 years ago; I expect that with my continued commitment it will be better tomorrow than it is today.

It is my hope to spare survivors of TBI and other life-changing injuries and illnesses a similar 30-year-period of denial. It is my wish to inspire them and their caregivers to develop more realistic dreams based on acceptance of what is and the realization that tomorrow can be better.

I know from my own experience that the family, friends and caregivers who were able to help me understand my limitations and reframe them into challenges that I could handle—into "realistic dreams"—were the ones with the greatest positive impact.

It takes great wisdom to know the difference between things we can and cannot change. Most of our frustrations in life arise from our unwillingness to accept the things we cannot change and our futile attempts to change the things we should accept. We harm others and ourselves when we fail to know the difference.

Acceptance into Action

The reality was that physical activity was painful. Did pain cause me to use the wrong muscles to walk, or did the fact that I used the wrong muscles to walk cause me pain? Either way, the answer was yes.

By finally acknowledging that walking was painful, I was able to begin a long journey of re-learning how to walk—in fact, learning how to crawl. With my therapists I discovered that the connections I had forged from my brain to my muscles very often made no sense. Ask me to move a toe and I would move an ankle; ask me to straighten an elbow and I would freeze: I had no idea. We spent hours deciding whether we should first remove the pain with an epidural or build up muscle functionality and strength to reduce pain.

Progress was slow, very slow; frustration was high. Physical therapists would tape my shoulders in place for a week at a time in order for my brain to learn where to hold them. The journey continues today. I continue to make progress; I have reduced my pain most days. I remain committed to a regimen of therapy that is designed to restore my life to its highest level of functionality. I could never have begun this journey if I hadn't been willing to accept that where I had been was not "normal." I was not OK. I was in pain. From that acceptance, progress was possible.

Precious Gifts

There is no training in our educational system about how to support our loved ones who are physically different, just as there is no training on how to be the best survivor that we can be. So we all must learn how to be ourselves around those who are "different," just as we must learn to accept ourselves when we are the ones who are "different." We must learn the patience to allow ourselves and others to be the best that they can be.

It is important to remember that everyone is entitled to their own definition of happiness. What looks terrible to an outsider may be okay to the person affected. After spending a week with my 86-year-old father, my initial reaction was to feel really bad about his quality of life. He, however, is very proud of his lifestyle and its quality. On second inspection, I realized I was judging him through my criteria. I had to remind myself to celebrate his happiness and put my judgment aside. It is hard, but it is rewarding.

I offer the following tips for helping the survivors of traumatic injury.

What TBI survivors need from family and friends:
- *Be yourself around me*
- *Share your hope*
- *Share your life with me*
- *Use past foundation to build tomorrow*
- *Be good company*

- *Laugh with me*
- *Don't help me wish for the past*
- *Love me as I am today*

How you will help me:

- *Teach me to be myself around you*
- *Teach me to have realistic hope (Bit by bit)*
- *Teach me to share my life with you (Listen)*
- *Teach me to enjoy past memories*
- *Teach me to enjoy your company*
- *Teach me to laugh at myself*
- *Teach me to live in the present*
- *Teach me to love myself as I am today*

My Realistic Dream Accomplished

Today I can be seen roller-blading six miles along the water-front, swimming at the athletic club, or doing Pilates with precision—none of which was possible 10 years ago—thanks to wonderful caregivers, helping me fulfill my passion to be a little better every day. Fifteen years ago, neither my caregivers, nor I, would have believed that I would be able to swim or roller blade; neither was even a goal. My goal was to be a little bit better every day—until one day swimming became an option. A couple of years later roller-blading became an option. Both were difficult. Both took incredible patience on the part of my caregivers, supporting me one step at a time.

Today I am in less physical pain, and my wife is in less psychic pain, than we have ever been in our married life together. I have the ability to play on the floor with my grandkids—something that would not have been possible 14 years ago. The gift of accepting my new norm, dropping the pretense that I was fine, is a win for my wife, kids, our grandkids and me.

I can now see that it was acceptance of my actual condition that gave me a realistic dream of reducing pain and improving my lifestyle.

As noted previously, it is my hope to spare other TBI survivors a similar 30-year-period of denial. It is my wish to inspire them and their caregivers to develop more realistic dreams based on acceptance of what is and the realization that tomorrow can be better.

There is a saying in psychology that summarizes the process we must take to progress. It is: "Face, embrace, erase." We must face and embrace our current limitations in order to change them. Many of us want to skip over the first two steps—which are painful—and proceed right to the third. I hope that readers will benefit from my 31 years of denial and realize that that approach simply does not work. We must accept (face and embrace) where we are in order to get where we're going.

I know from my own experience that the family, friends and caregivers who were able to help me understand my limitations and reframe them into challenges that I could handle—into "realistic dreams"—were the ones with the greatest positive impact.

Yours Can Be Accomplished as Well

We can help our injured veterans and other accident- and illness-survivors by modeling the courage to accept their current limitations. We can support and encourage their efforts to strive to improve each day. We can join them in celebrating each hard-won accomplishment.

We can support them in pursuing realistic dreams—dreams that give people a sense of purpose and a way to measure progress. We can be proud of their commitment to embrace each day as the first day of the rest of their lives.

We can all seek the understanding that enables us to separate the things we cannot change from the things we can, and the courage to change the latter.

It is my hope that all who have been touched by brain injury, military trauma, or any other life-threatening or serious illness, will find the strength to face a future that has deviated from their pre-event "normal." It is my further hope that, from that acceptance, will follow healing and change

It is my experience that you can make the injury the best thing that ever happened to you. I hope that you will—and that you will help others to do the same. You can do it!

Your Questions Answered

Just what is realistic hope? Realistic hope is really a simple and unique way of looking at the future by focusing on what you can achieve today. If every day you can make a little progress, who knows how far you can eventually go? More important, you will have the experience of success and satisfaction *every day* of the journey, instead of saving it all for the longed-for day when you finally "make it" to some lofty accomplishment.

Wouldn't that be limiting? No, just the opposite; it is empowering! I spent 30+ years trying to fulfill unrealistic expectations of myself and my family while we all were suffering silently. The satisfaction, the healing, the functionality and the resulting freedom that came as a result of accepting and addressing my actual physical condition and celebrating small accomplishments was incredible for everyone involved.

What about miracles? People tell me, "I don't want to cheat my loved one out of a miracle, as they do happen you know!" My response is that you increase the chance of a miracle by creating progress today to fuel the progress needed tomorrow. There's a saying that's apt in this situation: "Pray as if everything depends on God, and work as if everything depends on you."

But how do I know if the expectations I'm setting are realistic?" I think the biggest difficulty with setting realistic goals is one of timeframe. If I ask the question, "Will I ever walk again?" I'm asking someone to predict an indefinite future. This is something many have tried and most have failed to do. But if I ask the question, "Will I be able to move my foot tomorrow?" I have set myself a small but challenging goal within a definite timeframe—in other words, a realistic expectation. Once I have accomplished that small goal, I can build on it by setting another one for the next day, the next week, or the next month. Based on my progress at achieving these smaller, "bite-size" goals, I will be better able to set goals farther out. Perhaps one day I will be walking on my own.

What is the impact of not setting expectations, of just seeing what each day brings? It can be a real conundrum: if I set my goals too small, they do not count for much. If I set them too high, they cannot be achieved. Uncertainty results in paralysis and then the worst possible solution becomes the default: Don't set any! That leaves the survivor, the family and the caregivers each operating from different, unspoken goals and expectations—almost guaranteeing that they will each wind up frustrated. Each is measuring success in a different way! However, once you set your goals, you can adjust them tomorrow based on your progress today. You don't have to remain rigidly locked into them. Without expectations, there is no failure; but there also is no incentive, no motivation, and ultimately, no satisfaction.

But "realistic hope" is not very inspirational. I'm motivated by the end result—being able to walk, or swim, not "being able to move my big toe!" You can allow yourself a big goal to provide motivation, but break it down into smaller pieces so that you can measure success every day, or at least every week. These smaller accomplishments will give you the satisfaction and confidence to keep going. Ask your trained caregiver (your doctor, physical therapist, etc.) to help you establish reasonable small- and long-term goals.

For example, when I set a goal of learning to swim, my caregiver helped me break "swimming" down into the hundreds of individual skills I needed to acquire and then put together in order to finally swim. These included holding my breath under water; kicking my right leg; kicking my left leg; kicking them both in alternation; holding my body flat in the water; moving the right shoulder; moving the left shoulder; moving them both in alternation; and then finally, holding my breath and keeping my body level, while kicking my feet and moving my shoulders in alternation. Complicated stuff! And then I had to add turning my head to the left and opening my mouth to grab a breath with my left shoulder; then closing my mouth, putting my face back in the water, turning my head, opening my mouth, grabbing a breath with my right shoulder. It took me over a year to put all of this together—and was one of the most challenging *mental* tasks I ever accomplished!

Learning new skills today requires the same break-down of the larger task into its many components. The key is that I get to enjoy the feeling of success and accomplishment as I master each component task, rather than spend a year feeling frustrated and disappointed if that's how long it takes me to put it all together in the activity called "swimming."

What difference did realistic hope make for you? Over the years, my long-term caregivers would encourage me to "allow" my expectations to become realistic—in other words, allow my objectives to mature. Knowing it was counter-productive to oppose me directly, they were trying to gently slow my frantic drive to "get well" and "return to normal." Having a better grasp of how many bodily systems would have to be retrained, how many damaged neural pathways and twisted or atrophied muscles would have to be restored, or re-conditioned, they had a better sense of what was possible to achieve in a single day. But if they could get me to strive for something achievable, the satisfaction of accomplishing that goal would create the satisfaction that would fuel me for tomorrow.

Fifteen years ago, when asked to move a toe I would mistakenly move an ankle. Yet today I can do many complicated Pilates movements using the correct muscles. That's because my caregiver has the special talent of breaking each movement into small, achievable steps. I admire her for having the confidence and patience to lead me through 10 years of being just a little better today than I was yesterday. **What if my family members are the ones who are pushing me to set unrealistic expectations?** I hope you will find that setting and reaching achievable goals will fuel *their* confidence and satisfaction, as well as your own. Share this book. Although trained caregivers can help you know what expectations are realistic, survivors must do their part to work for—and accept—being just a little bit better every day. And friends and family members must also be patient and not expect their loved ones to "get back to normal" or "try harder" in order to make their own lives happier or easier. In the end, all of the people involved in your rehabilitation and recovery will influence your quality of life; and your progress and happiness levels will influence theirs, as well.

Do miracles happen? Yes they do, one step at a time. I am one of them. The journey is worth every bit of effort: The miracle sits on top of a great big pile of small accomplishments.

A lot of ground, where should we start?

Talk about longer term goals for the survivor – walk – swim – speak

Discuss the next steps to achieve that goal – move toe, get out of bed, etc.

Have a common shared goal among survivor, caregivers, family and friends.

Celebrate each success. If the steps cannot be achieved, redo the steps. If the step is too easy, increase the challenge.

Communicate plans, accomplishments and frustrations

Work for smiles, hugs and faith. Smiles for accomplishment, hugs for frustration, faith for the journey.

Afterword

Wow! This started out as a way to help others understand a void in the way we care for those who have suffered a traumatic brain injury. It turned to be a life-changing educational experience for me, as well.

As I shared the early drafts of this book with others, one by one, people would read the story and then start telling me their own stories—about similar experiences that remained painful or unresolved because of the mismatched expectations between themselves and the people who cared for them. They would also tell me how the book became a catalyst for change in their lives. As I listened to their feedback, I too began to revisit journeys I had forgotten and discovered what a traumatic impact my injury has had on my own family. My readers' willingness to "look in the mirror" prompted me to do the same. Thanks to their feedback, I am now a different person than I was when I started writing this book—just as my readers have told me they are different for having read this short piece of work.

What has become apparent is that none of us are ever trained to help our friends and family through a traumatic experience. At the same time, all of us want to help. So often the pain of being unable to help effectively compounds the pain of watching a loved one suffer. That's why I hope you will help me spread the word about realistic hope. Let's help teach each other how to help our loved ones when they need us most.

Thank you for investing your precious time in reading this book. I do hope that your return far exceeds your investment.

Readers Respond

"Will this be of benefit to helping brain injured and their families? A resounding YES! I found your approach to be most kind, caring and direct. Your personal experience obviously gives you a voice of authority."

* * *

"Never have I read such an easy-to-access step by step manual for dealing with a traumatic event. I think your book is probably THE handbook, not only for everyone affected by a person who has survived a TBI, but for those who have been the victim of a random act of violence, as I have. Humans are humans and all of us have the same, often unconscious, desire for the situation to return to normal so it can be relegated to the past. I hope all the people who need to read this will be able to."

* * *

"My mother was diagnosed with Lou Gehrig's disease 18 years ago and is still alive, although immobilized. My father felt it was his responsibility to be the caregiver for Mom out of a sense of shame from being away from the family in Vietnam during the '60s. This responsibility has almost taken on the form of epic martyrdom, to the detriment of his health and the mental health of family members. Many dysfunctional issues have gone unresolved out of an unwillingness to discuss the realities of this situation.

"After reading the book aloud to my parents and family members, many issues have been resolved and many more are being openly discussed, as opposed to being swept under the rug as if they did not exist. A miracle."

* * *

"As a caregiver I am always hesitant to share with someone recovering from a brain injury that it is important and okay to let go of who they used to be. Of course there is a period of mourning, but the faster they let go of the past there comes more energy to focus on the future. Many people are not ready to hear this and some are never ready. No one wants to talk about this with the person recovering because you can see how sad it makes them. Although with great care and empathy, I think I will be a bit more forward with this information. The book made me feel as if it is okay to do so."

Readers Respond

"I wish I had read this years ago—it would have made for an easier ride on a most difficult journey. In another situation now where my friend is dying of cancer, I am more certain when I am with her. I do not talk about what it will be like when she gets better. I do not speak as if she isn't really dying. Instead, I am with her and love her in the situation we are BOTH in now. I believe that is beneficial to her—that I don't ignore nor dwell on what is happening. I think we both benefit by sharing the time we have now."

* * *

"Thank you for this! I finished reading it and just put it in the mail for my Mom and Dad. Some of the advice can be hard to take for a survivor and their family/loved ones, yet you conveyed your message in a heartfelt way that I feel will be well received. There are so many people that I want to look at it."

* * *

"I reminded me of the difficulty people have when they try to change their behavior and well-meaning family and friends—who should be their greatest support—are often the largest inhibitors of the change. Learning to live with the "new normal" seems to go against human behavior, whether it is an intentional change or one thrust on us by a set of circumstances out of our control."

* * *

"I don't think you just wrote a piece on Traumatic Brain Injury. I think you wrote a piece on human behavior."

* * *

"I particularly like how you have defined realistic hope vs. unrealistic hope. I think people will be able to see themselves through those definitions and probably most people think they are doing right by placing unrealistic expectations on their loved ones.   It will be a good wake up call for them. The "Your support makes a difference" section is incredibly valuable. I would have given just about anything to have that list so clearly spelled out for me when I was managing care for my daughter."

Made in the USA
Charleston, SC
06 May 2011